Table of Contents

Introduction

Plans for how to solve the ills of a city are not in short supply. It is not uncommon for candidates, elected officials, and local leaders to develop plans and solutions in response to problems facing the community. Plans are good, the best of which lay out a road map for action and give a sense of direction. Unfortunately, too many of these plans consist solely of problems and solutions. Too many are simply a reflection and reaction to the current system, administration, or direction. These plans miss the mark because they fail to start at the beginning and determine the purpose and goals of the city and a long-term vision of how to achieve those goals. They also fail in another way: a diversity of opinion and lack of collaborative spirit. As the following pages will lay out, I believe that engaging the community in the governing process is one of the most important actions a city can take. It should be no different for the plans and policies that make up the vision for how that city should be governed.

So, while in the following pages, I humbly add to this canon with a strategy and specific policy proposals to help Tampa achieve the greatness its people deserve, this book is meant to serve as a spark to ignite a community-wide conversation about how we can make Tampa greater, together. I believe it is important to start with a vision and a set of policies and proposals on how to accomplish this vision. I hope those reading this will participate in those discussions and add to the vision and proposals that line these pages. These ideas and proposals will be archived on the accompanying website MakeTampa.com. You can also find more information detailing the process for proposal submission and dates of upcoming events on MakeTampa.com. It is my hope that from this centralized hub of ideas, a discussion and plans for action emerge that allow us to make Tampa greater, together. I thank you for reading Make Tampa and hope you will join me in creating a vision and playbook to help Tampa reach the great heights we know encompass its future.

Too often policies and proposals are created in a vacuum or as a reaction to some immediate problem. While individually these policies may be valuable, they often lack a sense of cohesion and long-term strategy necessary to achieve the macro goals of a city. Instead, there needs to be a fundamental understanding of what the policies are attempting to create. While different cities have different problems and varying needs, I would argue there are three basic elements necessary for the improvement of any city; attract and retain, create infrastructure and climate that allows for smart growth, and decrease the cost of government through efficient management. From these three core principles, specific policy proposals tailored to the unique challenges, needs, and opportunities of a city can flow. I will expand upon each of these in the rest of this section, before moving on to those specific policy proposals in the rest of the text.

It is often said that people are the lifeblood of a city. While the maxim refers to the passion and identity of a city, which is no doubt the case in Tampa, it can just as easily be applied to the finances of a city. Tampa derives revenue in a number of ways, from property and sales tax, to parking fares and business registration fees. The unifying factor in all of these revenue methods is that they are increased by the amount and activity of individuals in a city. A growing city is a strong city where people want to live, work, and play. As a City, we want to attract and retain the best and the brightest who will create and staff the jobs of the future. Smart growth can and should be a goal for the City of Tampa.

There are two ways in which a city can grow; attracting new residents and retaining existing residents. The latter of these is often neglected but is just as important. If a city is losing people at the same rate it is gaining people it is not growing. Both of these approaches rely on similar dynamics, mainly the attractiveness and desirability of the city. In Tampa we must create policies that further these goals. Focusing on quality of life, improved transportation, and strong empowered neighborhoods will help in the attracting and retaining process and should be at the heart of the City's policies.

Growth is important. Whether new residents moving in, new business created, or new building projects begun, a dynamic city is always growing and changing. As a city, it is important that we create an infrastructure that allows for, and encourages, this growth in a smart and beneficial way. We need to create an economic climate with minimal friction that gives the most opportunity to those starting and growing businesses in our community. Whether this is by removing obstacles to new industries and businesses, such as Uber and Airbnb; decreasing onerous regulations, or changing our code to allow for increased mixed-use development, we need to be focused on creating the opportunity for growth.

Government, like all organizations, can always operate more efficiently and drive down costs. It is all the more important in government because the costs come directly out of the pocket of its citizens. We need to implement a metrics-driven approach to make sure that we are operating as efficiently as possible. We need to work on being transparent so that the City can be held accountable to its goals and performance.

But how will we attract and retain, create the infrastructure and climate that allows for smart growth, and decrease costs through efficient management? I have laid out specific policies that I believe will help to accomplish these goals in the following chapters. These policies are broken out into three sections: Make Tampa Open, Make Tampa Thrive, and Make Tampa Seamless. While these sections are used for organization and the policies generally fall neatly into the specific groupings, there will undoubtedly be overlap and not every policy will fall perfectly into its designated section. However, the sections are important not just for the organizational benefits but also because they signify what I believe to be the three crucial needs of any city, including Tampa.

The first section, Make Tampa Open, focuses on how governments can operate more openly, more efficiently, and with greater engagement from the citizenry. Like any organization, cities can always improve on internal processes and external interactions. The City of Tampa can accomplish this by opening up its data, engaging and collaborating with the public, recording and publishing its vital metrics, and improving the governing relationship between the executive and legislative branches.

The second section, Make Tampa Thrive, focuses on the strategies and actions needed to develop economic growth in the City. It argues for a shift in thinking from an emphasis on corporate relocation and square footage based metrics to a focus on talent attraction and the incubation and support of local business. This can be accomplished by focusing on quality of life, infrastructure and transportation improvements, changing our code, and continuing to build a vibrant downtown core.

The final section, Make Tampa Seamless, focuses on a holistic approach to the City with an emphasis on strong neighborhoods and empowering our more disadvantaged communities. The title of the section borrows from the title of former St. Petersburg Mayor Rick Baker's book *The Seamless City* published in 2010.

The elements, policies, and proposals to achieve these three objectives are outlined in the following pages. Obviously, this is not an exhaustive list of proposals that would improve our City, nor should it be. Instead, the goal is to outline a strategy for the core elements of the process and to begin a collaborative discussion so that we can make Tampa greater, together.

Make Tampa Open

Opening Government to Collaboration

Politicians and elected officials are quick to trot out the oft-quoted bromide that citizens are the boss and that we are a government of the people. Unfortunately, all too often the sound bite is as far as the sentiment goes. There is a misconception among both elected officials and citizens that somehow those governing have some extra wisdom or know better than those governed. The truth is that elected officials, appointed officials, staff, and the rest of the individuals that make up the government are no different than anyone else in the City. We do ourselves a disservice if we fail to tap into the collective thoughts, wisdom, and ideas of the citizenry to make Tampa a better city. By empowering citizens and unleashing this collective wisdom we can take Tampa to great heights.

As the Co-founder and CEO of Citizinvestor, a leading provider of civic engagement and crowdfunding tools for local government, I know the difference that policies that empower citizens to invest in their community can make.

I also have the pleasure of serving on the City's Citizens Advisory Budget Committee (CABC). The committee is comprised of seven members (each appointed by one City Council member) tasked with reviewing the budget, meeting with department heads, and providing feedback and recommendations to the Council. The CABC is a great opportunity for the Council to hear from non-elected citizens and has resulted, in my opinion, in many positive actions for the City.

But what if instead of seven voices, the Council and Mayor could hear from 70, or 700, or the whole populace?

The City has taken some positive steps in this direction in the past with the InVision Tampa project and the City's hack-a-thon. The results from these undertakings were eye-opening, offering new insight into Tampa residents' ideas and vision for the City. Projects like these are important beginnings in seeking out more information and opinions from the community. The City must go further and embrace open government, not as a series of one-off projects, but as a built-in ethos that permeates the governing process. Specifically, the City needs an open data policy and a focus on crowdsourced government.

With the opening of data into organized and readable formats, we have seen tools ranging from crime mapping to bus tracking popping up across the country. Imagine the possibilities that could be created in our community if instead of a three-day hack-a-thon, data was made available on an ongoing basis. Cities across the country are creating open data standards to do just that and Tampa can be on the forefront of this trend.

On a daily basis the City takes in a large amount of data across all departments. As citizens we are familiar with some of this data, particularly the crime statistics broken out by neighborhood. But there are reams of data being collected continuously that would be similarly enlightening to the public. This includes everything from building permit applications and fulfillment times, to park attendance, to parking patterns. All of this information is important and the public should have access to it. However, it is not enough to simply provide the information. Instead it needs to be organized, searchable and in easily accessible formats.

Opening the City's data has several benefits. It provides information to citizens about their government, encourages participation in building citizen-led solutions, and creates accountability on the part of the departments providing the data.

The amazing thing is that open data is the exception and not the norm. If government truly works for the people, then shouldn't the products and information behind that work belong to the people? The data is simply a recording of the interactions between the citizens themselves and their government. This is enough of a reason, in its own right, to enact an open data policy. But there are additional benefits that come out of this openness. A city can tap into the collective imagination and creativity of the populace. New solutions and tools can be created by a citizenry begging to be included in the governing process. We have seen the impact made from solutions created during three-day hack-a-thons, let's build this into the fabric of our governing process.

Implementing a process in which departments are releasing data on their performance creates a sense of shared accountability that will make the City more efficient and effective. Departments will get better at tracking their metrics and will have real-time feedback on how they are performing. This will not only incentivize better performance but will allow for quicker changes and improvements to be implemented based on actual information.

Opening up data to provide the information citizens need to create new tools and solutions is a great first step in improving the governing process, however, it is not enough. The City has to embrace and want to collaborate with these citizen-led initiatives. There has to be a commitment to the understanding that governing should be a collaborative process.

This process can and should take many forms in multiple outlets to encourage the most engagement. This can be online engagement platforms similar to the InVision project implemented by the Buckhorn administration or online reporting tools like what St. Petersburg implemented through SeeClickFix. What these tools have in common is that they make it easy for people to take part in the governance of their city, through idea generation and issue reporting. This type of engagement creates a sense of ownership, participation, and commitment to one's community. It also improves the services that a city provides. However, this increased engagement also needs to occur offline to provide access and availability to all citizens. This should take the form of more issue-specific town-halls and community meetings that allow for wide-scale participation by being scheduled at convenient times and locations for the public to attend. These meetings should be geographically diverse to encourage participation throughout the City of Tampa.

Providing these outlets for increased engagement and communication between citizens and government is only half the battle. It is equally, if not more, important to have a process by which this input is consumed, internalized, and ultimately implemented by the City.

Measure Everything

We must build on, and extend, the work started by the Buckhorn administration in 2015 with the Performance Measurement Dashboard. The current dashboard is a good start, but it must be extended to include all departments. We also must, as described in the previous section, open up the underlying data that makes up the top-line metrics. Tracking and displaying this type of data on municipal services and performance is important for two reasons. First, it creates trust and furthers engagement with the citizenry. Individuals are able to quickly and easily track how we are performing as a government, where improvement is needed, and where positive progress has been made. We can no longer ask citizens to simply trust government, but instead must show them in real time how we are performing. Second, creating real-time measurements to track performance and progress improves decision making at the department level. The impacts from changes in strategy or staffing can be measured in real time allowing departments to double down on those bearing success and pivot away from those that aren't.

The City should make a commitment to have all departments participate in the government dashboard. If displaying these real-time metrics builds trust in government, then the goal should be to make the application citywide across all departments. Not only will this build more trust, but it will also allow all departments to experience the same improvements in decision making and enhanced accountability. The City can and should move from a small sample of metrics-driven performance data to a full program across all of City Hall. This change in the culture and ethos of City government will build trust with the public and improve efficiency and impact across municipal services.

It is not enough to simply release the top-line metrics of performance without also releasing the underlying data sets that the metrics are based on. It is too easy to manipulate data with the right graph or chosen sample and for the public to fully trust these metrics the underlying data also needs to be released. Aside from the increased trust element, a focus on the underlying data will give departments a better understanding of the factors affecting the top-line numbers. This will allow for more informed and quicker decision making. Finally, the release of the underlying data will allow interested citizens to build tools and solutions to improve services based on real-time data. In order for us to ingrain metric-based decisions into the culture of City Hall, we must commit to the production and release of the underlying and top-line metric data.

Lean Startup for Government

One of the best-selling books in the startup world is *The Lean Startup* by Eric Ries. The idea behind the Lean Startup Process outlined in the text is that companies should build a minimal viable product (MVP), which is the "version of a new product which allows a team to collect the maximum amount of validated learning about customers with the least effort." Companies should then get immediate feedback from actual users on this product and iterate, or make changes, based on the feedback. This process should be repeated over and over until the product is desirable to customers. The benefit of this approach is that hypotheses can be tested quickly and with real-time feedback, and companies can avoid the costly mistake of spending precious time and resources building a product that ultimately won't be accepted by the public.

This principle is important because, unfortunately, it is the exact opposite of how government works. In government there is a fear and cautiousness associated with new and innovative projects. This leads to endless studies and large investments in time and capital before a project is ever released to the public. There are multiple problems with this approach. First, especially with the pace of technology and advancements, by the time these large-scale projects or updates are released, they are already outdated. Second, the projects are based on guesses or hypotheses about what will work without any data or real-world testing to back them up. And if they are unsuccessful or less successful than planned, there is a real reticence to change course because of the time and resources spent. This leads to a lot of suboptimal projects and a less efficient and innovative government culture.

Instead, the City should, when possible, seek to mirror the lean startup model by releasing small pilot programs. These pilot programs can be released quickly, tested with measurable results, and improved before being released to a larger segment of the public. This pilot-based iterative process will save resources, both time and money, on the front end and improve results and quality on the back end. It will also allow new technology and innovative approaches to be utilized and tested. This approach goes hand in hand with the government dashboard. The key is to identify measurable results and metrics that the program is seeking to accomplish before the program is implemented. These early hypotheses can then be tested through cheaper, scaled-down programs to determine if they actually accomplish the expected results. These pilots can then be rolled out to the public at large, iterated and re-tested, or scrapped, based on the performance and data. And like the open data and government dashboard proposals, this would have the additional benefit of increasing transparency to the public.

This innovative approach needs to be built into the fabric of City governance. The goal should be to have every department engaged in this pilot-based testing approach. However, like all new innovative approaches, there is a learning curve and a degree of expertise necessary to implement this system. For this reason, a new department should be created, modeled after the Office of New Urban Mechanics in Boston and Philadelphia, to help facilitate this citywide innovation. In keeping with the lean government principles laid out in this section, the department should start small, with one position. In fact, it should be revenue neutral by reclassifying one position from the current Innovation and Technology department. This new position would report directly to the chief of staff and act as a liaison and internal champion for innovation and lean government experimentation within City Hall.

Working with Council

The Tampa Charter sets up the City's governance in a strong-mayor format. In practical terms, this means that the Mayor has wide authority and discretion in the governance of the City, with the Council's main responsibilities being the approval of the budget and zoning matters. It is important for there to be a strong voice and leader to create a vision and implement that vision for the City. However, it is also important that that leadership be balanced and enhanced by a strong voice from the City Council. Council members represent a voice for their constituents and provide valuable insight and ideas that can only strengthen the City. With that in mind, there are three policies that I believe would enhance the working relationship between the executive and legislative branches of the City and increase the accountability of the Mayor. First would be a quarterly meeting where the Mayor would answer questions from the Council in a public forum, similar to Prime Minister's Questions in England. Second, the Mayor should have monthly meetings with each Council member. Finally, the budget process should be reformed to allow for greater input and feedback from City Council.

With the strong-mayor form of government that the Tampa Charter lays out, it seems incongruent that the public can see the deliberations of the City Council on a weekly basis, but rarely has the same opportunity to see the Mayor. Similarly, when the public does see the Mayor, the occasion is typically a ribbon cutting or prepared speech. The public would benefit, and the Mayor would retain more accountability, if there were regular opportunities for the Mayor to answer questions from the public, through their elected representatives on the Council. This policy would also allow the Council to have a larger impact, which would emphasize the checks and balances necessary for good governance. A balance between access and accountability and the importance and limited nature of the Mayor's time needs to be struck. In that vein, a quarterly Mayor's Questions, limited to no more than one hour, would be an ideal approach to creating more access and accountability.

While these quarterly public forums that allow for Council members to question the Mayor are important for access and accountability, it also is important for more informal meetings to be held to increase cooperation and partnership. These meetings often do occur when a contentious or district-specific issue arises, but they are too reactive and sporadic. A better approach would be for the Mayor and Council to make a commitment to meet one on one on a monthly basis. These meetings would allow for more proactive conversations and better long-term cooperation and partnership.

Reforming the Budget Process

The budget process needs to be reformed to allow for more input from the Council. While the current process gives the appearance of a check and balance approach between these two branches of government, in reality the Council has little to no input in the final budget. The current process entails the Mayor drawing up a budget and delivering it to the Council, who then have only one month for review. For all practical purposes the Council really only has two options, to approve or deny the budget. Sure, there is an initial public hearing and speeches are given, but in the end the budget is approved almost entirely unchanged. This process removes the vital input from the Council, as proxy for the public, that is sorely needed.

The process should be fixed in three ways. First, there should be multiple public hearings in the months leading up to the Mayor's proposed budget that allow the Council and public to voice their respective budget priorities. Second, the Mayor should release the proposed budget no less than two months before the final vote is taken by the Council. And third, the first vote on the budget should happen earlier in the budget cycle to allow for a realistic potential of a denial of the proposed budget and time to reform for approval.

The budget is the driving force behind all decision making and resource allocation. Every citizen is touched and affected by the makeup of the budget. For this reason, it is vitally important to allow citizens to voice their input, not after the document has already been solidified, but during its construction. Similarly, the Council, with their focus and understanding of their respective districts, should be involved while the budgetary decisions are being made. This input can be accomplished through public hearings scheduled prior to the unveiling of the proposed budget. These hearings should take place late enough in the budget year that there are revenue projections to help guide the discussion, but early enough that they have an impact on the final proposed budget.

While input on the front end is important in helping to shape the proposed budget, there also needs to be change in the timing of voting on the back end. The public hearings provide the opportunity to influence the proposed budget, and the approval vote guarantees the ability to influence the final budget. However, if there is no real threat of non-approval, then the impact is in name only. To change this, and give the approval process the power it is intended to have, the proposed budget unveiling should be moved up as well as the voting on that budget. These changes will give the Council the time necessary to review the budget and if changes are needed, to deny the proposed budget in time for the changes to be made to obtain approval. The priorities and allocations of the budget are too important to exclude input from the public and Council that is necessary to produce the best possible document.

Make Tampa Open by:
- Creating an open data policy and open data standards for City data
- Releasing data in organized, searchable, easily accessible formats
- Establishing policies for departments to release data related to defined performance metrics
- Having more issue-specific town-halls and community meetings that allow for wide-scale participation by being scheduled at convenient times and locations for the public to attend
- Establishing real-time metrics to track performance and progress
- Committing to the production and release of the underlying data along with the top-line metric results
- Embracing a lean startup approach to government by implementing small pilot programs to test potential solutions
- Creating a new department modeled after the Office of New Urban Mechanics in Boston

and Philadelphia to help facilitate citywide innovation

- Implementing a quarterly public meeting in which the Mayor would answer questions from the City Council
- Establishing a routine of monthly meetings between the Mayor and each City Council member
- Reforming the budget process
- Holding multiple public meetings before the budget is released for citizens to voice their ideas and priorities for the budget
- Releasing the proposed budget earlier in the cycle to allow more time for review
- Moving up the time of the first vote to allow for more input from the Council before the final vote

Make Tampa Thrive

Economic development is one of those terms that is widely used, broadly applied, and rarely understood. Plainly, it is the process of developing, nurturing, and improving an area's economy. But this explanation too is ill defined. How does one determine the improvement of an economy, what measurements should be used? These pages are not the place to argue economic definitions. Instead the focus should be on the goal of the City's economic policy. Our economic development should seek to foster an environment that attracts and retains the best and brightest while also encouraging the creation of high-paying jobs and the production of local goods and services that attract capital from around the country and world. Fostering the type of environment and infrastructure that allows for these changes will help the City of Tampa achieve the level of economic development we strive for and deserve.

The most important resource for any business is the quality of its workforce. In Tampa we have a great labor pool, from our strong public schools, to our quality higher education institutions, to the work ethic that flows through our citizens. We need to build on these strengths and work to attract and retain those individuals who make up this quality workforce. These individuals will both attract the companies that will create jobs as well as create the startups and new companies that will build the economy of the future. These new growing companies and our strong existing companies will build the goods and services that will attract outside dollars and capital to our community.

Cities, like Tampa, are not just competing with the old versions of themselves, but with cities across the country. People have more and more flexibility in where to live and work and are constantly making decisions about the best place to inhabit. This competition for talent must always be at the forefront of our thinking.

Unfortunately, most of our current economic development focuses almost exclusively on corporate relocation. That is not to say this type of activity does not have value and the potential for job creation. But focusing on it as the main piece of economic development is problematic because it often leads simply to a trading of corporate headquarters. Too often the relocation only lasts as long as the sweetened deal and then the company relocates to the site of the next incentive package.

This type of corporate headquarters trading is inefficient and does nothing to build a foundation for future success. It is also an outdated approach that ignores the changing dynamic in today's workforce. More and more workers are independent from physical offices and instead working remotely. We can see this in the new business models that are emerging in our economy and the changes brought on by improvements in technology. This will only continue in the future and Tampa needs to tailor our economic development in kind.

Therefore, attraction will come not from the physical structures but from quality of life improvements that attract the best and brightest. This economic development strategy de-emphasizes the incentive and relocation approach and instead focuses on the attraction of talent and creating the atmosphere to allow for local businesses to succeed.

The focus of our economic development strategy should be on attracting and retaining the type of skilled workforce that will build and attract the companies we want in our community. The best way to accomplish this attraction and retention is to focus on the things that are important to these types of workers, mainly quality of life, infrastructure and transportation, and downtown vibrancy. Tampa can and should be seen as a place with a great quality of life, a high caliber infrastructure and transportation system, a thriving downtown, and improved land use.

Quality of Life

Quality of life is often used as a catch-all term for all of the elements that go into the experience of living in a particular area. This makes sense and the quality of one's experience is made up of many disparate moments and experiences. In fact, almost everything that is laid out in these pages goes to the quality of life experience to the citizens of Tampa. However, for purposes of this section, I am focusing on two specific areas: public spaces and parks, and education.

Public spaces and parks are often an underrated aspect of the experience of living in a city like ours. Whether a playground where you take your children, a quiet spot under a tree to read or gather your thoughts, or a gathering place for community building, these spaces are of vital importance to our City.

While there have been many improvements in the City of Tampa in the last five years, probably the most noticeable and impactful has been the transformation of the downtown core. The strength and attractiveness of a city's downtown core is integrally important to the overall health of a city. There is a whole section in this text dedicated to the improvements of downtown for just this reason. However, I note it here because a large part of the change in downtown was brought about by three public space/park projects: Curtis Hixon Waterfront Park, the Riverwalk, and Water Works Park. These three projects have brought a walkability and attractiveness to downtown. They have also, like all great public spaces, created a connection point for a wide range of citizens to congregate, interact, and enjoy the beauty of the City. These spaces become a destination, creating a draw to the area and allowing attractions and restaurants to grow and thrive around it. We need to push for more of these types of open spaces in the downtown core. We must also work to connect these spaces with a focus on more pedestrian-friendly walkability that links these parks and open spaces into an integrated network.

This focus on public spaces and parks is just as important in our neighborhoods as in the downtown core. Playgrounds, parks, and open spaces can serve the same connective purposes for the various communities of neighbors around the City. We need to work on not just creating more and better parks and open spaces, but also making sure that these spaces touch every corner of the City. It should be our goal to have a vibrant public space in each and every neighborhood. These public spaces need to be easily accessible and pedestrian and bicycle friendly. Parents shouldn't have to get into their car to find a playground or park for their kids to enjoy. Nor should they feel unsafe in walking or biking to the area. To ensure this equality of access, the City should commit to a plan to guarantee every citizen lives within walking distance or a public space or park by 2020.

Building and maintaining public spaces is one of the best ways a city can improve its quality of life. The access to and enjoyment of these spaces is what young people, families, and citizens of all kinds are looking for when they make a decision to move into or stay in a community. This quality of life improvement will bring and retain the workforce that will attract the companies and jobs we want. This increase and improvement of parks and public spaces should be a critical element to our economic development efforts.

Improving and creating new public spaces and parks needs to be combined with an increase in the programs and offerings attached to the parks and spaces. This is especially true for those programs aimed at our youth. After-school programs and sports leagues provide an outlet for constructive activity and a place for kids to feel supported. These programs are opportunities to instill values and help build life skills. The City recently took a promising step in this direction by expanding programs and keeping parks and facilities open later. We need to build on this and continue to work to offer more opportunities for these programs.

It is not just youth programs that make an impact on our City. Quality structured programs can complement our parks and open spaces by providing places for people to meet and connect. These connections create a greater sense of place and increase the quality of life in the City.

Throughout time, a distinguishing characteristic of great cities has been the culture and art that permeate through and radiate out from them. A city's art, like its public space, helps create an identity and sense of place for people in the community. Public art, be it outdoor sculptures, murals, or even a lit-up building or bridge, is key to creating an inviting and desirable city. The City of Tampa has many of these public art assets and we should continue to build on these to make Tampa a leader in public art. We need to empower our artistic community to reimagine our public space and buildings. These actions require little in the way of costs to the City, but much in the way of imagination. Improving our public spaces and parks, expanding our programs, and increasing the quantity and quality of our public art will go a long way in improving the quality of life in our City and attracting and retaining the individuals who will help make Tampa the city it can and should be.

Education

It goes without saying that education is one of the most important issues facing our country. And while it is true that education policy is created at the federal and state level, and implemented at the county level, that doesn't exclude a role for cities. This is especially true because the quality of a city's education is important not just in attracting new people and companies to the area, but also in raising up the next generation of leaders in our community.

The quality of our education system is one of the great challenges we face as a nation. At the local level education policy and execution is the responsibility of the Hillsborough County School Board. However, this does not mean that the City of Tampa does not have any part to play in making our schools the best they can be. As together we work to make Tampa greater, it is vital that we educate, encourage, and develop the leaders of tomorrow. There is no substitute for a strong educational foundation in our children. The quality of our schools is also vital as a recruitment tool for corporations and the best and the brightest we are seeking to attract. Businesses routinely list the quality of an area's schools as an important factor when determining where to relocate. This follows with the earlier discussion on the move towards business following talent and not the other way around.

Two steps that Tampa can take to help improve education in our City are incentive programs for municipal employees to participate in mentoring at our schools, and joining together with private donations to create a supplemental fund for teachers and principals.

Mentorships are a vital part of the education of our youth. All of us have benefited and learned from a mentor relationship, whether a family member, a teacher or coach, or a more formalized mentoring program. We need to make sure that the children in our community have as many opportunities to experience these mentor relationships as possible. One step in helping to cultivate this is to show leadership at the governmental level. The City can create an incentive program to encourage municipal workers to participate in mentoring programs. This leading by example can help to encourage mentorship from the populace at large and make it an ingrained part of the culture.

While increasing access and opportunities to mentorship, we can do more to support the work of the most important mentors: teachers. The education of our youth, and the economic development advantages that come with it, is incumbent on the great work of our teachers. The City can work with private entities to create a supplemental fund to reward teachers and principals and to help with the acquisition of the tools and supplies needed for a twenty-first century education.

Infrastructure/Transportation

We are a city on the rise and are building a reputation as a top destination in the Southeast. While much of this reputation reflects our vibrancy and growth, we also, unfortunately, have become known for an unacceptable amount of pedestrian and bicycle deaths over the last few years. These deaths are not only tragic for their loss of life, but are indicative of a planning process that focuses too much on cars and not enough on walkability. Study after study has shown that young people are moving away from car ownership and use. This is all the more prevalent as our urban core continues to grow in population and density. We need to embrace this changing dynamic and focus on building and expanding networks of walking and biking paths and connections. This is done in two ways: allocations of funding in the budget, and design and planning decisions.

Over the past couple of years, we have seen more of a focus on building dedicated bike lanes in the City. This is a good first step, but it is still just a drop in the bucket of the changes that need to be made. The approach has been too reactive and scattered. Instead, biking and pedestrian walkways should be at the heart of our City footprint. With the existing assets we have in place, from the one-of-a-kind Bayshore Boulevard, to Curtis Hixon, and the resurgent and emerging neighborhoods of Ybor and Channelside, we have all the potential for a world-class city built on walkability. We also need to move beyond the downtown core and push for more bike lanes to connect neighborhoods from Port Tampa to USF.

Focusing on biking and pedestrian safety and on the walkability of our City is important to improving the quality of life of our citizens and in attracting the best talent from around the country. It is also important to our transportation issues. We need to provide options and opportunities for people to move away from only car use. Whether this is through new innovative approaches like car sharing or improved public transportation, a vital component is the ability to walk or bike in a way that is safe and convenient.

We truly live in an age of innovation. Nowhere is this more apparent than in the sharing economy inhabited by companies such as Uber and Airbnb. These companies, and companies like them, are having huge impacts on how people travel, work, and live. This is especially true in urban environments such as Tampa. Unfortunately, another thing these companies have in common is that they are being stymied by outdated and often hostile over-regulation. Nowhere is this over-regulation and failure to embrace innovation and the changing economic landscape more apparent than in the Public Transportation Commission's (PTC) attitude towards ride-sharing. Hillsborough is the only county in the State of Florida that operates a regulatory commission like the PTC, although other counties have been similarly hostile to Uber and other ride-sharing services. This innovative approach to transportation provides more options and service consistently rated better than taxis, and has been shown to decrease instances of drunk driving. Yet the PTC has made every effort to stymie ride-sharing. Unfortunately, this approach is not just due to a lack of foresight and apprehension about innovation, but also the all too common instinct for government to protect incumbents in the market. When an incumbent, in this case taxis, begins to lose ground in a disrupted market, government and regulation is often the last refuge.

The issue goes beyond one company or one industry, but an approach to new innovative companies and a changing economic landscape. We should seek to be a leader in integrating these companies into our economic structure. This will not only benefit our citizens by offering new and improved goods and services, but will also attract the companies that will be creating the jobs of tomorrow.

The constant street flooding that the City is exposed to is an all too stark reminder of what has become apparent the last few years: our stormwater infrastructure is inadequate. Our City becomes gridlocked with South Tampa taking the brunt of it. This must change.

As a member of the Citizens Advisory Budget Committee, I have had the opportunity to analyze this issue in depth. In fact, the committee put a recommendation in both the 2013 and 2014 reports to address this stormwater infrastructure issue.

It should be noted that the Stormwater Division, especially over the last couple of years, has exceeded expectations in its ability to stretch and utilize its limited resources. The infrastructure has been neglected for too long and the issues are too numerous to be solved overnight. However, while much of the recent conversation often focuses on the amount of resources available, the more important issue is the allocation and use of those resources.

Our current system emphasizes short-term, quick-fix maintenance over longer-term, structural solutions. Unfortunately, this decision is forced on the department by the fee allocation system Tampa uses. Under this system, the stormwater fee is allocated only to maintenance and therefore any funds raised from bonding must be used solely for that purpose. This leaves a big hole in the funding needs. It also is a lost opportunity to fund the type of capital investments that could lead to the long-term structural fixes necessary to solve the flooding issues we continually experience.

A solution to this problem, and the recommendation that has been made by the Citizens Advisory Budget Committee, is to split the fee so that a portion can be spent on maintenance and a portion on capital improvement projects. Under this setup, bonds could be issued for both purposes. This would give the Stormwater Division the necessary resources to be able to permanently solve issues instead of continually doing quick Band-Aid fixes and save money in the long run. A split of this kind would need to be initiated by the City Council, and should be in order to solve our flooding issues.

Downtown Vibrancy

The strength of a city is often measured by the vibrancy of its downtown core. This makes sense as downtown is typically the first place tourists and newcomers visit. The downtown core is also a natural gathering point for citizens. The goal of any downtown is to maximize the live, work, and play options that attract individuals and businesses alike. Creating this vibrant core that is a center of job creation in the day and a lively entertainment district by night is a constant, continual process. Much improvement has been made on this front in downtown, whether the emergence of Curtis Hixon and the expansion of the Riverwalk, to the Mayor's Food Truck Fiesta, and farmer's markets popping up across downtown. This is an improvement I have seen first-hand working downtown for the last three years. I chose to locate my company,

Citizinvestor, downtown because of this growth and development and it continues to be a strong selling point for attracting talent to our company.

As a city we need to continue to build on the gains that have been achieved downtown. We can expand the attractions that have been developed, from the Mayor's Food Truck Fiesta to the varied events that take place at Curtis Hixon. We can and should focus on building on the cultural assets, improving the walkability and rideability of the downtown core, increasing mixed-use development, and improving transportation options. As downtown is the focal point of our City and the initial impression for outsiders, we must continue to build on the momentum that has been achieved downtown. A strong, thriving, and vibrant downtown is a key to making Tampa the world-class city we know it can be.

Improving the Building Codes

The physical look and feel of a city is impacted by what can be and what ultimately is built. These decisions are based on rules and regulations set up in a city's building, zoning, and development codes. These codes are hugely important to the development and growth of a city. While the public often sees elected officials and leaders making decisions on a project by project basis, the decisions are governed and influenced by these codes. It is important we have the best possible codes in place as we build and shape Tampa into the city it can and should be. Part of ensuring we have the best codes is by moving towards more form-based code.

The Form-Based Code Institute provides a good definition of form-based codes and the impact they have on public space:

> "A form-based code is a land development regulation that fosters predictable built results and a high-quality public realm by using physical form (rather than separation of uses) as the organizing principle for the code. A form-based code is a regulation, not a mere guideline, adopted into city, town, or county law. A form-based code offers a powerful alternative to conventional zoning regulation."

The City of Tampa's Planning and Urban Design Division is currently working on moving towards more form-based code. This is an important step for the City and one that needs to be pushed and executed to ensure the best possible planning process.

Increasingly people are moving to live, work, play centers that allow individuals to experience everything a city has to offer without needing to get in the car or travel long distances. As a city we need to embrace this trend and increase and utilize mixed-use development. This is one reason why form-based codes are an important step in the development process. This type of mixed-use can be seen in our downtown core where the population has greatly increased over the last few years. People of all ages are moving to apartments downtown where they can just as easily walk to their favorite restaurant or park as they can to their office down the street.

We need to continue this type of mixed-use development downtown and also increase mixed-use in other parts of the City. This development not only helps attract people looking for that live, work, play destination, but it also helps in creating the walkable and rideable city that we want. Another aspect of creating this type of environment is changing our approach to parking.

One of the enduring features of our car-centric culture has been the influx of parking minimums into our development codes. It is understandable that a city would want to make sure that new stores and housing units have parking, however, these minimums have a negative impact on a city as a whole. The three biggest downsides of this extra parking are a negative impact on walkability, a decrease in available space for housing units, and lastly a general unattractiveness.

Recently the New York University Furman Center did a study that showed that more parking spaces are built because of parking minimums than would exist based on market conditions. These extra spaces are inefficient and decrease the available space for other usable, revenue-producing development. Space is a limited resource, especially in the denser areas of our City. We need to maximize and use the space as efficiently as possible.

The excess of parking also goes to the imbalance between automobile traffic, and walkability and rideability. Part of correcting this imbalance to focus on making Tampa a model for walkability is to move away from strict parking minimum requirements. Removing some of these spaces opens up areas for bike lanes and pedestrian throughways. It also increases the visibility of street-level attractions and improves outdoor dining.

Finally, as we move to improve our codes and encourage mixed-use development, decreasing the overabundance of parking, and inefficient allocation, the visual quality of the City will improve.

Make Tampa Thrive by:

- Committing to a plan to guarantee every citizen lives within walking distance of a public space or park by 2020
- Increasing structured programs from the parks and recreation department
- Becoming a leader in public art by empowering our artistic community to reimagine our public space and buildings
- Creating incentive programs for municipal employees to participate in mentoring at our schools
- Joining together with private donations to create a supplemental fund for teachers and principals
- Splitting the stormwater fee so that a portion can be spent on maintenance and a portion on capital improvement projects
- Removing onerous regulation and barriers to innovation to allow companies of the new economy like Airbnb and Uber to thrive
- Continuing to focus on downtown vibrancy by building on cultural assets, improving

walkability and rideability of the downtown core, increasing mixed-use development, and improving transportation options

- Moving to a more form-based building and development code
- Encouraging more mixed-use development
- Moving away from strict parking minimum requirements

Make Tampa Seamless

We have seen tremendous growth in our downtown core over the past five years. This is important. A strong and vibrant downtown is an economic development engine and attraction for the people we want to recruit to our City. This is why I discuss downtown vibrancy above in the economic development section. However, there is an issue when this focus becomes overwhelming and takes away from neighborhood development in the rest of a city. Rick Baker, the former Mayor of St. Petersburg, published a book on his time governing the city a few years back titled *The Seamless City*. That title, along with his elegant description of the problem and solutions, has stuck with me. Here is how Mayor Baker described it in the opening of the book:

> "In a seamless city, when you go from one part of town to another, you never cross a seam — whether a street, interstate overpass, or railroad track — and enter a place where you do not want to be ... where you feel the need to reach over and lock your car door; an area with boarded-up

buildings, broken windows, and large tracts of urban blight, with drug dealers on the street corner.

"All parts of the city are not the same, and that will always be true. Some areas have large houses and big lots, while others may have duplexes and apartments; but all parts of a seamless city should have certain things in common. They should be safe and clean and should have the services, retail, and public infrastructure that adequately accommodate the people who live there.

"A seamless city is an attitude that we are all in it together. It means that we do not pit one area against the other, but work toward advancing the entire city by addressing the needs of the parts. ... It's connecting everyone with bike paths, and encouraging the community to gather together at dog parks and playgrounds.

"A seamless city looks for ways to help the homeless turn their lives around while not allowing them to adversely impact others, and has a downtown that becomes a gathering place for all who live there. Such a city works with neighborhood leaders so that the residents define and help execute their own ideas for progress. A seamless city also understands that our public schools are not islands to be left drifting on their own. They are vital to the city's success and should be supported by everyone.

"No area in a seamless city should be crime ridden and blighted. All of our children should grow up in neighborhoods that are safe and clean; that have libraries, parks, athletic fields, banks, shopping centers, and grocery stores; and where every boy and girl can share in the pride and success of the entire city!"

— Rick Baker, February 7, 2011

While part of the same region, Tampa is not St. Petersburg and the challenges, opportunities, and assets we have differ, but the desire to create the type of seamless city Mayor

Baker describes should color our efforts. We too should want a city that is united. A city where economic development, quality of life, and public safety are not limited to certain areas or neighborhoods but instead extend to the entire city. We should want a city with strong, unique neighborhoods, each with its own identity but also imbued with a sense of cohesion as an important and integral part of the City of Tampa. Every citizen should feel not only comfortable, but proud of where they live. We need policies that build on and support our neighborhoods, encourage economic development in all parts of the City, and provide access to municipal services for all citizens.

Strong Neighborhoods

There is a famous quote attributed to Abraham Lincoln that says "That which governs closest to the people, governs best." The sentiment behind this quote is that the individuals closest to the issues and problems facing their community have the best insight into the solutions needed. This is true for states compared to the federal government, cities compared to state government, but also neighborhoods compared to a city at large. This is the reason we have district council members, because we think they will have more insight into their area than elected officials that don't live in the district.

One of the great aspects of our City is the strong, diverse neighborhoods that populate our area. These neighborhoods are unique in their aesthetics, culture, and makeup, but also, often in the issues and opportunities that they face. We should embrace this by allowing each district to retain a small percentage of property tax revenue to spend on issues and opportunities for that district. Setting aside a small amount of tax revenue to be kept and spent in the district allows for input and a sense of ownership on spending priorities. It also allows for more accountability by bringing the spending decisions down closer to those whose funds are being used. This approach will allow our individual neighborhoods and communities to make spending decisions that will help make Tampa the place our citizens deserve. We can also formalize this involvement through a new Neighborhood Council.

One of the great institutions of civic involvement we have in this country is the neighborhood/civic association, and in Tampa we are blessed with a strong stable of neighborhood associations. These organizations of civic-minded citizens are a window into the wants, needs, and concerns of the citizenry at large. City government needs to embrace this opportunity to tap into the wisdom and passion of these dedicated groups. Unfortunately, these associations are too often only engaged when a problem occurs or when a new policy needs to be sold. This reactive, top-down approach wastes the opportunity that these groups provide. Instead these citizens should be embraced to help build and structure policy.

In fact, the embrace should be formalized in a Neighborhood Council that reports directly to the Mayor through the Mayor's chief of staff. The council would be made up of one representative of each of the City's neighborhood/civic associations. Each representative would be elected by the members of their association and would serve staggered two-year terms. The council would meet monthly to discuss issues and priorities for their various neighborhoods and the City as a whole. Members of the administration would be present to answer questions, provide feedback, and listen to issues of concern. Yearly, the council would prepare a report for the Mayor. Our neighborhoods are the backbone of our City and the dedicated civic-minded individuals who put their time into bettering their neighborhoods deserve a voice in the governance of the City. This involvement will help to continue to make Tampa a city of connected, strong, vibrant, and unique neighborhoods.

Enterprise Zones

One of the great urban policy successes of the past thirty years has been the creation and implementation of Enterprise Zones.

Tampa's Enterprise Zone is comprised of several geographic areas that have been targeted by the State of Florida for economic development. The program promotes community revitalization and job creation within the Enterprise Zone through tax credits and refunds. These Enterprise Zones are a great policy to encourage economic development in otherwise underutilized areas of our City. It is important when looking to create a Seamless City that the focus is empowering all areas both with a voice in policy, as described above, but also through increased economic development.

The City of Tampa can supplement the incentives offered by the State of Florida with Tampa-specific incentives and additional benefits. A municipality thrives when all of its parts thrive separately and together. Through the addition of Tampa-specific incentives we can encourage even more economic development and community revitalization in these underutilized areas of our City.

Access to Services

Making a city feel seamless applies as much to people living and working in every neighborhood and corner as to those who are visiting. This means that every citizen of the City of Tampa should have, as we have discussed in earlier sections, thriving neighborhoods, strong schools, and economic development opportunities. But they should also have access to City services and a connection to the government that represents them. Part of that access is created through the openness and transparency that is outlined in the first two parts of this book.

An additional way to increase access is by bringing services out into the community. A great example of this approach has been the Boston City Hall to Go program, outlined below in an excerpt from an article in the Smithsonian Magazine:

> "One experiment that has been replicated in several other places is Boston's City Hall to Go, a mobile truck derived from the success and popularity of food trucks, that now

stops in neighborhoods and offers direct access to civic services, like requesting parking permits and paying property taxes. The 'mobile City Hall' offered 50 services and completed 4,050 transactions by the end of 2014, leading to similar programs in Vancouver, British Columbia and Evanston, Illinois."

This is an approach that can be replicated here in Tampa. This is an inexpensive way to make City services more accessible. Beyond the continued focus on our online solutions, this physical embodiment of the City traveling to individual neighborhoods can have a real psychological impact on those in neighborhoods that feel underserved. Opening government and increasing access helps to make Tampa a place where all citizens feel connected, appreciated, and important.

Make Tampa Seamless by:
- Allowing each district to retain a small percentage of their property tax revenue to spend on issues and opportunities for their district
- Creating a Neighborhood Council that reports directly to the Mayor

- Expanding empowerment zones
- Improving access to services through a City Hall to Go program modeled after Boston

Conclusion

In concluding, I would be remiss if I did not expound and clarify the title of this book. Some critics, and even some readers, may ask, why do we need to Make Tampa, isn't Tampa a pretty great place to live as it is? To that I would say, of course. We have all chosen to live, move to, or stay in Tampa because it is a great city. And it is because of this greatness that we must demand more. We must make Tampa together. Making is a collaborative process that builds upon the foundation we have and constantly strives for better.

Together we can make Tampa more open by more vigorously tracking performance metrics and releasing this data to the public. We can begin to transform government into a more open process through crowdsourcing and new technology. We can make government more responsive and accountable by improving the budgeting process and creating a new Mayor's Questions initiative. Openness, accountability, and more input from the public that it serves can only improve the quality of our City government.

Together we can make Tampa thrive by changing the way we think about economic development. Instead of solely focusing on trading corporate headquarters with other major cities, we can make Tampa the number one destination for the talent that will attract and create the businesses we want and need. We can increase and improve our public spaces. We can focus on pedestrian and bicycle safety and access. We can improve the look and feel of our City through improvements in our code and by removing parking minimums. And we can continue to focus on building a vibrant downtown. These changes will help make Tampa a world-class destination to attract and retain the talent that will help create and attract the jobs of the future.

Together we can make Tampa seamless by focusing on our strong neighborhoods. We can empower our neighborhoods to help in the governing process. We can increase and improve access to municipal services. And we can incentivize and improve the economic opportunities in the less affluent neighborhoods of our City. A seamless city is a stronger city and together we can make Tampa seamless.

Governing can and should be collaborative. While I feel strongly that the strategy and policies I have laid out in these pages are important in moving our City forward, this is merely a first step. The goal is to create a conversation that leads to engagement and the fashioning of a long-term plan to make Tampa the greatest city it can be. I encourage everyone who has read these pages to visit MakeTampa.com and add your input, ideas, and analysis. By tapping into the collective spirit and passion of an engaged citizenry, we can make Tampa greater, together.

About Tony DeSisto

Tony DeSisto is an entrepreneur and attorney, passionately working to make Tampa a better city. Tony currently serves as CEO of Citizinvestor – the world's largest crowdfunding platform for government projects with more than 185 city partners. Tony co-founded the company in 2012, while serving on the City of Tampa's Citizen Budget Advisory Committee, where he served as Vice-Chairman. It was on this committee that Tony saw the need to create a new form of civic engagement, where citizens could work together with City Hall to propose, prioritize, and fund projects to improve their community. Tony is an active member of Tampa's startup community, investing in and advising some of the area's fastest growing companies. Passionate about investing in his community, Tony has served on numerous boards and committees for state and local government. Tony also leads his own law firm which specializes in municipal law. Tony received his JD from Stetson Law School and his Bachelors in Economics from Bates College. Most importantly, Tony is a husband to Courtney and father to Trajan, Nali, Teddy, and Titus.